DOGTOWN

A Sanctuary for Rescued Dogs

Published by Sellers Publishing, Inc.
P.O. Box 818, Portland, Maine 04104
For ordering information:
(800) 625-3386 toll free
Visit our Web site: www.rsvp.com • E-mail: rsp@rsvp.com

President and Publisher: Ronnie Sellers
Publishing Director: Robin Haywood
Editor-in-Chief: Mark Chimsky-Lustig

ISBN 13: 978-1-4162-0526-5
Library of Congress Control Number: 2008928020

10 9 8 7 6 5 4 3 2 1

Printed and bound in Canada

Best Friends®
ANIMAL SOCIETY

DOGTOWN

A Sanctuary for Rescued Dogs

by Bob Somerville

Introduction by Michael Mountain
President, Best Friends Animal Society

SELLERS
PUBLISHING

GREGORY

Contents

LEE

BUBBA

Best Friends Animal Sanctuary, at the heart of southern Utah's national parks, is home on any given day to some 2,000 abused and abandoned dogs, cats, and other animals. As the word sanctuary implies, Best Friends is a haven for these animals—the largest no-kill sanctuary in the country. In addition to taking animals from other shelters and rescue groups, Best Friends employs its own Rapid Response teams to conduct rescues after natural disasters and other major events that put animals in jeopardy. Dogs with special needs, such as those from closed-down puppy mills or dogfighting rings, benefit from Best Friends' expert medical, evaluation, and training programs at Dogtown, the canine section of the sanctuary. In 2007 Best Friends was entrusted with the care and rehabilitation of 22 of the dogs rescued from their painful lives with Michael Vick. Many of the rescued animals need just a few weeks before they're ready to go to good new homes; others who are sicker or older or have suffered extreme trauma find a home at the sanctuary for the rest of their lives.

Best Friends reaches out across the nation and beyond to help bring about a time when there will be no more homeless pets. Working with other humane groups, Best Friends helps communities establish spay/neuter, foster, and adoption programs so that every dog or cat who's ever born can be guaranteed a loving home.

BOOGIE

LAURA

EURO & KEA

WYLIE

Introduction

Love Unlimited

by Michael Mountain, *President*, Best Friends Animal Society

Angel Canyon, the home of Best Friends, is a miracle of nature, millions of years in the making. What happens here every day, for thousands of homeless animals, is a miracle of love.

It's a miracle made possible by the thousands of people who share with us the simple belief that kindness to animals makes a better world for all of us.

Much of what happens to animals in today's world is not kind. They're treated badly in dogfighting rings, and in puppy mills, where mother dogs spend their entire lives in small cages churning out the cute puppies you see for sale at pet stores. They often can't even get the help they need when they're rescued from abusive situations and taken to a local shelter.

Best Friends is here to make a difference in all that. It is a wonderful place for animals, with healing magic all its own. Our veterinarians comment that the place itself often does as much for these once-sad little faces as can be done for them medically. The clean, dry air, big open spaces and warm blue skies are the perfect backdrop to the animal homes here — and especially to Dogtown.

And "Dogtown" isn't just a fun name. From the very beginning, it's always been a town. Dogs are social animals. They naturally form their own societies and their own hierarchies with their own codes of behavior. Dogs who have been treated badly need to rediscover their own true nature, to become real dogs again. So they need to be with each other in order to do that.

Of course, we can't bring all the abused and abandoned animals in the country to Best Friends. When the sanctuary was getting started in the late 1980s, more than 17 million homeless dogs and cats were being killed in shelters every year. And as more and more people got to know about Best Friends, the sanctuary became the flagship of a growing movement to bring an end to the killing of homeless pets in shelters everywhere. This no-kill movement, with its emphasis on spay/neuter and adoption programs, has already brought that number down to fewer than 5 million a year.

Indeed, the two kindest things any of us can do for homeless dogs and cats is to adopt our pets from shelters, rather than buying them from pet stores, and always to have them spayed or neutered.

On a larger level, puppy mills are now being exposed, and more and more of them are being shut down by local authorities, as are dogfighting kennels. Of course, that means that the four-footed victims need somewhere to go when they're rescued. Dogtown is always busy developing new model programs that will help shelters and humane groups care for the abused and abandoned dogs they're taking in.

Many of these new programs focus on the mental and emotional healing of dogs. Just like us humans, traumatized dogs and other animals have scars on the inside just as they do on the outside. And just like humans, they can't get better physically while they're still suffering mentally and emotionally. This is one of the most important aspects of the work that's going on these days at Best Friends' Dogtown.

Another thing that makes Dogtown so special is the number of visitors, volunteers, and vacationers who spend time here—more than 25,000 each year. Some drop by for a few hours on their way to one or another of the national parks close by. Others spend a few days or a week or more. A few stay forever!

Needless to say, the dogs love it. They love being taken for walks, groomed, hugged, taken back to hotels or motor homes for a sleepover, and having people make a big fuss over them. Best of all, it helps them get ready for new homes—which is always the ultimate goal.

Most recently, some of the dogs, along with the people who care for them, have become the subject of a new series, *Dogtown*, on the National Geographic Channel. You can meet these new "stars," and most of the other dogs, too, on the Best Friends Web site at www.bestfriends.org. And while you're there, you can also find out how you can help bring your own neighborhood closer to a time when there will be no more homeless pets.

None of the work of Best Friends would be possible without the hands and hearts of people like you. Thank you for caring about them—and for making it all possible.

Two of Dogtown's octagonal dog shelters display their architectural grace against the stunning backdrop of Escalante National Park's bold escarpments (far right). The dog-runs in each octagon house four or five dogs apiece; dogs of a similar size, such as the pointers and hunters above, are often grouped together, but the prime concern is compatibility. At right, caregiver Bonnie sets out with a motley crew for a morning walk.

The Story of Dogtown

In the predawn quiet, desert birds begin to sing. Wild turkeys stir from their perches in the canyon's willows, where they have spent the night safe from coyotes. A gentle breeze sets hundreds of wind chimes ringing in the memorial grove called Angel's Rest. And as the sun peeks above the canyon rim, the dogs of Dogtown stretch and rise, ready for another day. The cycle begins again at Dogtown.

For some, this will be an ordinary day, full of good times with their companions, walks and treats from caregivers and volunteers, grooming and therapeutic exercise, and long, peaceful naps in the shade of junipers. Some will be coming back from a sleepover with a visitor who just might be that special person they've been waiting for. Others will be arriving at Dogtown for the first time, probably a little anxious as they get checked by the vet and start to explore their new surroundings. And for others still, this will be their last day at Best Friends, as they head off to their new forever homes.

Dogtown bustles with activity every day. Its buildings and play areas teem with canine antics of all kinds, and if you stop and talk to any one of the caregivers or volunteers who keep things going, you'll quickly learn the place is filled with wonderful stories as well. Dogtown itself has a good story, but so does every single one of its inhabitants.

RUTH

18

A Tale of Two Worlds

The contrast sometimes boggles the mind and at the same time touches the heart. Esther, Moses, and Ruth, gorgeous golden short-haired mixed breeds, had lived all their lives in a prison defined by the length of the chain each one of them was hooked to 24 hours a day. Looking into their big liquid eyes, it's hard to imagine how any human could so mistreat them—never walking them, never interacting let alone playing with them, never taking them to the vet, barely remembering to feed them—but that's the way it was for Ruth, the mom, and her two pups Moses and Esther. And then things took a turn for the worse. Their people decided they were too much trouble, and were arranging to have them put down. Fortunately, a rescuer intervened and made arrangements to get the dogs to Best Friends for special care.

Best Friends isn't like other shelters, where people just come by and leave unwanted animals. It focuses its efforts on special cases—dogs who need the kind of care that only Best Friends can provide. Indeed, the sanctuary develops approaches to health and behavior care that can then become models for the rest of the animal protection world. So most of the dogs at Dogtown come from shelters and rescue groups. While individuals can apply to have dogs placed at Dogtown, the sanctuary receives hundreds of such applications every week and can accept very few of those. Moses, Ruth, and Esther were lucky enough to be in that number.

Now they found themselves ensconced in a new world called Dogtown where they were encouraged to socialize with other dogs to break the mold of negative behavior that chaining often causes.

Ruth went to one of the pair of octagon buildings known as The Garden, in Dogtown Heights; Esther went to Conrad and Leopold's in the oldest part of Dogtown; and Moses joined The Clubhouse, also part of Dogtown Heights. Their new homes were a combination of indoor and outside space that's the signature of Dogtown's octagons. The only chain was the chainlink fence

MOSES

19

ESTHER

enclosing some 5,000 square feet of running room, dirt to dig in, and shade trees to lie beneath. Their caregivers were delighted at how quickly each of them adapted to the wholly new concept of freedom. And everyone could see the smiles on their faces as they tromped around outside, coming up to the fence to greet visitors.

Moses made a big impression on a visitor named Nicole, who had come from Connecticut to vacation-volunteer at Best Friends. She watched him go through his first minutes and hours of adjustment, enjoyed how quickly he seemed to be fitting in . . . and then found herself falling in love. She signed up to take Moses back with her that night to one of the guest cottages at the sanctuary for a sleepover and ended up taking him the three more nights she was going to be there. At the end of her week, she applied to Best Friends to adopt Moses.

Less than a month later, Moses was again happily ensconced, this time in Nicole's home. Nothing speaks more eloquently of Dogtown's role in dogs' lives than when the stay is brief. Dogtown folks talk about the sanctuary as being a temporary home before dogs move on to their forever homes, but they deliberately hold on to that word "home." Dogtown for so many hundreds and even thousands of dogs has "happy" all through it: they are happy to be there, and happy to leave.

In the Beginning . . .

The story of Moses, Esther, and Ruth paints a good picture of Dogtown as it is today, its state-of-the-art facilities providing precisely what any kind of dog in need requires. These three learned to make new friends, living in divided sections of the octagons that hold about four or five dogs each; in some cases, though, a dog may need personal space, a puppy may need more constant monitoring, or an older or smaller dog may need closer human contact. Dogtown can accommodate them all.

And it can handle every type of dog personality as well. "Dogtown is like any other town," says Faith Maloney, one of Best Friends' founders and the person in charge of Dogtown during its first 10 years. "It has characters of all kinds: serious types like you might find downtown at the chamber of commerce, clowns and exhibitionists who enjoy making a spectacle of themselves, students who are figuring out where they fit into the social order, and some who are physically or emotionally challenged and need a little extra

PRECIOUS, whose back was broken not long after she was born, was brought to Dogtown's clinic for evaluation and care. The little Rottweiler mix was soon fitted with a special harness and two-wheeled cart so she could get around. Dogtown's medical staff doesn't give up on dogs with even such severe problems, knowing they're still capable of a happy life. Precious was adopted before she turned six months old and now lives with her new best friend, a dog named Helen.

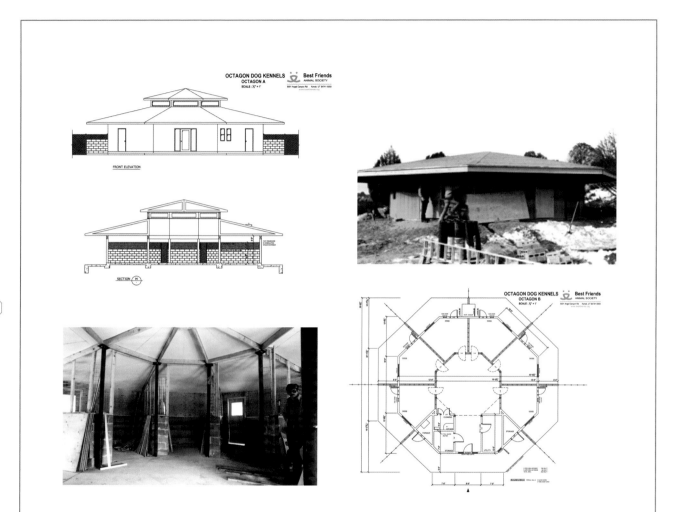

The first octagonal dog homes at Dogtown took shape in 1987 (top right). Seen from the interior (bottom left), a standard octagon included separate indoor enclosures and a central hub from which caregivers could monitor all the dogs. In the late 1990s, donations made possible more sophisticated versions of the octagons, shown here in designer blueprints. A higher ceiling over the hub improves lighting and ventilation, and each indoor enclosure now includes better access to an outdoor play area. The eight octagons of Dogtown Heights have a standard pattern and are grouped in pairs. In each pair, one octagon has six dog runs and the other, four.

help getting around. It's a rich, vibrant community."

There is nothing like Dogtown anywhere, but it wasn't always such an elaborate, multifaceted place. Its roots were fairly humble. The whole thing started with a group of friends, several from the United Kingdom, who had found themselves drawn to the American Southwest and to the mission of saving homeless pets from abuse and abandonment. They worked closely with their local humane societies, saving as many of the animals as possible who were scheduled to be put down for lack of good homes. In the late 1970s a few of them gathered together enough money to buy a ranch near Prescott, Arizona, where they established their first, small sanctuary to rehabilitate these so-called "unadoptable" dogs and cats and then place them in good homes. But they were constantly on the lookout for a place that was bigger and better — and, they readily admit, a place with a touch of something deeper to it. It had to feel right.

A few years later, Francis Battista, one of the group, was driving from Arizona to Salt Lake City when he passed by a glorious-looking canyon off Highway 89 a few miles outside Kanab. On a whim, he drove in. No harm in asking. As he turned down a dirt road that ran beside Kanab Canyon, he knew almost immediately that he had found the right place. He called Michael Mountain (now Best Friends' president) and told him the news. "It used to be a movie ranch where they filmed the TV series *The Lone Ranger*," Michael says, "and famous movies like *The Outlaw Josey Wales* and *How the West Was Won*. By the time we found it, Hollywood had gone home. It was the most scenic place I could ever have imagined." Soon the whole group of friends had assembled to discuss the matter, and again pooling their resources, they bought the 3,700-acre lot in the summer of 1983.

Hard work followed, clearing brush, building rudimentary structures, putting in pathways and a road or two. Some of the team remained in Arizona and kept that shelter going until things were up and running in Kanab Canyon—which, seeking a more appropriate name, they had rechristened Angel Canyon. Eventually they were able to move the whole operation north, but there was still much to be done. They had mostly dogs with them, and some cats, who could initially be cared for in people's homes. But the dogs needed their own space. It would be Dogtown, a name that seemed to come to Faith almost out of the blue—as had many of the signs that had led them to this place. Before they had even begun to lay out a site on the sanctuary for Dogtown, Faith was thinking about the structures for housing dogs. She had seen a program on a sanctuary in California that employed octagonal buildings—a design that allowed caregivers to monitor several different enclosures and play areas fanning out from the central hub. It would become the defining characteristic of Dogtown.

The first three octagons were completed in 1987, and 150 dogs soon took up occupancy. They included the Sheriff of Dogtown, Amra the Malamute, and his girlfriend, a petite mutt called Rhonda. Amra was a giant good-ol'-boy sheriff, slightly on the plump side and always happy to help people go around the system … in exchange for a small gratuity, payable in biscuits. One of the sheriff's main duties was conducting tours. As he and Rhonda took visitors around, other canine residents often joined the walk, because all paths led to Ginger and the Federal Reserve Tree.

Ginger, a Chesapeake retriever, would do the rounds of Dogtown twice a day, collecting the tennis balls that the other dogs had been playing with and piling them up under what the founders had come to call the Federal Reserve Tree. There she would conduct her afternoon banking operations and reconcile her "accounts." Once Ginger had collected the balls, other dogs would come by and put them back into circulation. Tennis balls were clearly the currency of Dogtown. Wealth was apparently measured by how many they'd gathered up or were playing with on any given day. But Ginger always got them back—although she never hoarded them. It was all about keeping the economy vibrant—giving away the currency, then calling it back in, and sending it back out.

By 1992, Best Friends Animal Sanctuary was still in its infancy, but Dogtown had already become a complex society. Some

SPUDS goes for a walk with Mary past the Dogtown headquarters, which also houses the clinic. A very popular "sleepover" dog, Spuds was adopted once, then returned because he didn't get along with one of the female dogs in his new home. Best Friends insists that adopting families return a dog if things don't work out. For Spuds they eventually did: he was adopted again, this time for good.

25

GUARDIAN, 10 years old, lives with two other shepherd mixes at Old Friends, the part of Dogtown Heights reserved for pooches "of a certain age." Typical shelters don't give older dogs much time to be adopted, so they rarely fare well. At Dogtown, older dogs get however long they need to find a forever home, and on average more than 50 are adopted a year. One visitor wrote of Guardian: "He is gentle, relaxed, affectionate, playful with toys, housetrained, sweet, strong, but well-behaved—an absolute gentleman!"

of the dogs, like Amra and Rhonda and Ginger, had been there for a couple of years or more. Others were coming in from all over the country as Dogtown's reputation grew as "the place" for dogs who had suffered serious abuse, neglect, and trauma to start a new life. Simply being at Dogtown was central to the healing process. Most of the dogs needed expert medical care. But they also needed to be with their own kind, to run around in the fresh air, find their place in a canine hierarchy, and socialize with each other before they could begin to build confident relationships with humans again.

Dogtown continued to expand, as did the whole sanctuary, over the next few years. One of the most important additions was on-staff veterinary care, but there were physical improvements as well. In 1997, early benefactors Homer and Dolores Harris put up $500,000, challenging the growing number of Best Friends members to match the amount, so that a much-needed addition to Dogtown could be built, and that's the new suburb called Dogtown Heights ("A Gated Community"). Today, new additions to the neighborhood include Old Friends, for older dogs; New Friends, home to rescued puppies and their mothers, many of whom have been saved from puppy mills and backyard breeding operations; Pittie City for the 22 "Vicktory" dogs who came to Best Friends in the wake of the horrific case of former NFL star Michael Vick and his dogfighting kennels; The Lodges, for dogs who prefer to be in pairs; the Laundry Room, where some small, mostly toothless, funny-looking

SEYMOUR enjoys a plush, carpeted spot atop an industrial-strength washing machine in Dogtown's Laundry Room. He and half a dozen or so older, smaller dogs get to hang out in the laundry, which provides a safe refuge from stronger, younger canines who might bully them. Little ones like Seymour mingle with the staff and get the kind of loving attention that makes older dogs feel secure and not left out.

27

old geezers like to make themselves comfortable among the piles of clean, warm laundry that keeps coming out of the dryer on a chilly day … and many more.

Some of the dog homes, like Homer and Dolores and Jeffrey's Place, are named after people who donated the funds to build them. Others, like Maggie's Mercantile, recall famous canine founding fathers and mothers.

Snaking through all these facilities are numerous pathways where volunteers and staff take dogs for walks, and nearby is a fenced-in dog park where dogs get a chance to meet and play.

Three other buildings play crucial roles in Dogtown's functioning. The headquarters building includes the clinic, where all Best Friends' animals get medical care, and attached to it is Admissions, which has 14 kennels where newly admitted dogs can

CARLA, WOODY, AND NORM, known affectionately as the Pupsicles, fit neatly in the hands of a member of Dogtown's medical team while their mom, Diane, looks on. The three pups and Diane were found on a property in Utah in the dead of winter—Diane chained up and her newborn puppies out of her reach, lying frozen on the ground, near death. The aptly named Pupsicles bounced back quickly at the Dogtown clinic and went on to do their growing up at New Friends, Dogtown's center for puppies. After weaning her pups, Diane was adopted.

28

DIANE

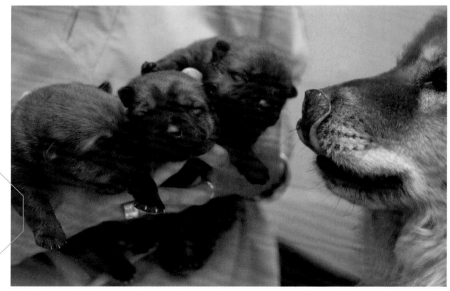

be evaluated by the medical staff and trainers, who will decide the best place for a particular dog to live. A color-code system lets everyone know what's what. Family-friendly dogs get green collars; dogs who are friendly but who are not approved to be around children get purple ones; dogs with special medical needs get yellow collars; and those who have displayed aggression to people or other dogs get red collars. It is the stated goal of all the staff to try to get those red-collared fellows to green, and it's something the caregivers never give up on.

Tara's Run is the place where such works-in-progress get a chance to take a meaningful step toward adoption. Named after the family dog of a Best Friends member, it's an enclosed training center that includes an obstacle course for agility training. Best Friends' trainers work here with all the dogs who need to learn behavioral skills. Some of the dogs who end up at Dogtown, for example, have never seen a set of stairs and just have no clue how to negotiate them, so Tara's Run includes steps they can practice on. Because no dogs live in Tara's Run, it's a great neutral ground for introducing a prospective adoptee to a dog who's already part of the adopting family.

And finally there's the Fitness Center. It's a state-of-the-art facility dedicated to the health and wellness of all Dogtown's dogs. Its most impressive feature is undoubtedly the hydro tank, where dogs with arthritis or an injury can get low-impact exercise that can vastly improve their mobility. But it also has a grooming station, giant "fur" dryer for just-bathed pooches, and numerous other physical rehabilitation features.

29

SOLDIER enjoys some exercise time in Dogtown's Fitness Center, swim-walking in the hydro tank. Born without a front left leg and a deformed right front leg, Soldier was abandoned, left tied to a tree. Hydrotherapy kept him fit despite his immobility, and Soldier was eventually adopted by a psychiatrist, who employs him as a therapy dog for children. Soldier is now part of an experimental program to develop state-of-the-art prosthetic limbs.

Spotlight on: Porto

One fellow who benefited from the Fitness Center—as well as from the care of Best Friends' team of vets and vet technicians—is a lovable big Labrador mix named Porto. He was removed from a neglectful home in Washington State and put in a shelter, but he wasn't doing very well. He had terrible skin problems that had left him with almost no fur on his body, and he was badly underweight. The local shelter didn't feel they could do anything to help him, and he was on the way to the sad fate that befalls so many shelter dogs across the country. But a vet who had checked on him had been touched by his sweet nature, so she agreed to foster him. A member of the military, she was called up to active duty in the veterinary corps and got in touch with Best Friends to see if they could help since she would no longer be able to keep him. He was just the sort of special case Best Friends likes to reserve room for.

Porto came to Dogtown clearly in need. He had earlier been diagnosed with demodectic mange, a parasitic skin infection that can be extremely itchy and can also lead to secondary skin infections. This type of mange is normally only seen in puppies, but Porto's malnourishment and neglect had apparently stressed his system enough to bring it on. He was assigned to the healing expertise of Dr. Michael Dix, Best Friends' medical director, who

When Porto first arrived at Dogtown, he was miserably itchy, suffering from a severe form of mange that had left him almost completely hairless and with secondary skin infections (above). Dr. Michael Dix, head of Best Friends' veterinary clinic, prescribed medications that helped rid him of infection; Dr. Mike also fitted him with a special collar to prevent him from scratching his raw skin further, and a body-hugging tank top to guard against sunburn (right).

continued some of the treatment Porto was already on—a drug to eliminate the mites causing the mange, and antibiotics for the secondary infections. He also tested to see if Porto had any allergies that might be exacerbating his condition.

PORTO

The thing that got to everybody was what a good dog Porto was. He knew all the basic commands, would give a paw when asked, and would jump for joy when he was excited to see someone. Vets, caregivers, and volunteers alike couldn't help but love him. The allergy tests, for example, required taking four vials of blood from the carotid artery in his neck, hardly a pleasant procedure. "Porto acted like a dream patient," says Dr. Mike, "calmly sitting perfectly still for me, portraying no distress or discomfort." It's hard not to think he knew it was all for his benefit.

Porto was fitted with a special kind of neck cone—it looks more like a brace—to keep him from scratching his raw skin, and a stylish white tank top to protect his body from sunburn. He was given antibacterial medicated baths, and his ears, which had developed an infection, were also treated. Most dogs squirm when getting ear treatments, but again Porto would sit patiently and let it happen. As the healing continued, he started putting on needed pounds weekly, and a good diet along with plenty of play time with his new doggie friends helped restore his muscle tone.

Porto had been in Dogtown a few weeks when a woman named Nita came to volunteer, spending a fair amount of time with the dogs in his run. When she returned home to Pennsylvania—

to a house with two dogs and two cats—she found she just couldn't get the lovable Porto out of her mind. So she applied to adopt him. Not long after, Dr. Mike got the results of Porto's allergy tests: it turned out he was allergic to many things outdoors, including grasses, trees, and weeds. He could be treated for this, so Dr. Mike agreed that he could be adopted. Nita was overjoyed, and after she brought him home, she was brimming with good reports. "When he sees his leash it is too funny," she wrote back to his friends at Dogtown. "He jumps a foot in the air and wiggles. If he gets too excited, I just say 'relax' and put my hands up slightly and he immediately sits down, trying to contain himself. He waits patiently when I change his t-shirt, almost as if to make sure I don't forget."

Porto's fur will likely never grow back in completely, and he may have an odd, patchy appearance the rest of his life. But Nita reported a few months after first adopting him that a passing car had stopped and the driver had shouted what a beautiful dog he was—and Porto wasn't even wearing his stylish tank top. "He has such a kindness about him," Nita wrote, "and everyone who meets him loves him."

Dogtown had worked yet another miracle—or, perhaps more to the point, it had allowed the miracle of this dog's own resilient nature to thrive. "The thing we do so well," says Faith Maloney, "is to create a real life for dogs. Dogtown is a rich world that enables every dog to reach his or her full potential—a world where they can leave behind whatever they've suffered and create a new life that makes up for everything that went before."

A DOG'S BEST FRIEND

Trainer Extraordinaire

ANNIE

"She has a remarkable knack for getting inside an animal's head," says one of Sherry Woodard's colleagues about Best Friends' dog training and animal behavior expert. Indeed, whenever there's a case that needs special handling, Sherry's the first one called—and they called her when Annie came along. Annie, who's playing ball with Sherry at left, had gotten in serious trouble for biting a child in a neighbor's backyard, and her family was about to euthanize her even though Annie had always been loving and gentle. She was saved, though, and delivered into Sherry's capable hands. Sherry started intensive evaluation and training of Annie, whom she found delightful. Through Sherry's careful guidance, Annie was able to make it past the one bad incident in her history: after a brief few weeks living with her Dogtown pals, she was adopted.

One moment with a dog named Sassy also exemplifies the brilliance of Sherry's work. Sassy was painfully shy and went into fits if anyone but her owner was around. Sherry began a series of simple socialization exercises introducing new people to Sassy. After a while, the dog got more and more comfortable but she had a setback near a crowd, raising her hackles and growling. Without a second thought, Sherry got down and embraced Sassy, wrapping her arms around her. "I was keeping her from practicing threatening behavior by moving her through that space with physical and emotional support," says Sherry. It was an intuitive but insightful reaction. Sassy calmed right down, and they continued to make great progress.

33

One of the several thousand dogs Best Friends rescued in New Orleans after Hurricane Katrina swims toward help (far right). Lennox (foreground, above) and BeBop enjoy an off-leash run near Dogtown; tastes of freedom do wonders for dogs saved from crisis by Best Friends' Rapid Response teams. Michelle Besmehn, Dogtown's manager, hauls supplies to Little Lebanon, the temporary annex established at the sanctuary in 2006 (inset).

Rescue, Recovery, Renewal

From Crisis to Comfort

Dogtown has thrived as a sanctuary and as a waystation to better the lives of thousands upon thousands of dogs over the years. But where do all those dogs come from? Best Friends is not your typical shelter or animal rescue organization. Its mission is to respond to the wide world of companion animals in crisis. When Hurricane Katrina struck New Orleans and the city began to flood, Best Friends knew that dogs and other pets would be left in the wake of the catastrophe, and its staff and members and other volunteers responded on the ground.

Temporary tented shelters called yurts, play areas, and supply vans cluster near the edge of a Best Friends horse pasture where staffers established Little Lebanon—first home for the 150 dogs rescued from the fighting in Beirut. Many of the materials used to build Little Lebanon came from the Tylertown sanctuary set up by Best Friends 100 miles north of New Orleans after Hurricane Katrina.

As Michael Mountain, president of Best Friends, explains, "We rescued and transported 6,000 dogs and cats and other animals—almost half of the entire number of animals who came out of New Orleans after Hurricane Katrina." Best Friends responded again less than two years later when bloody fighting broke out in Beirut and elsewhere in Lebanon, and again when a deadly earthquake hit Peru. Sometimes Best Friends steps in when dogs are the direct victims of abuse and neglect. In recent years, Best Friends' commitment to rescue and to their no-kill principles has nowhere been better represented than in the case of the most infamous dogfighting ring in the nation, which had involved football star Michael Vick. As in so many instances, Best Friends answers the bad news of cruelty and abuse with the good news of providing a safe place for rescue, healing, and love.

Spotlight on: The Vicktory Dogs

The story hit front-page news headlines late in April of 2007: a 15-acre property in Virginia owned by Atlanta Falcons starting quarterback Michael Vick had been found to be the scene of a major dogfighting ring. At first it seemed Vick's own involvement might be merely tangential, as he claimed. But as the news developed over the next few days and weeks, it became clear that Vick had played a significant role in the operations of the ring, known as Bad Newz Kennels, apparently after a nickname for Vick's hometown, Newport News, Virginia. By August, Vick had pled guilty to felony dogfighting conspiracy charges and also admitted taking part in the execution of several dogs by hanging, drowning, and other means that horrified the vast majority of the American public. He would eventually be sentenced to 23 months in prison.

More than 60 dogs were removed from Vick's property in Virginia, some badly wounded from the fighting itself, others in clearly traumatized states. One was deemed by the authorities to be too aggressive to be handled at all and was euthanized. But more than four dozen of them were able to be housed temporarily in local animal shelters. Meanwhile, a highly charged debate was under way in the nationwide animal protection community.

Some of the best-known humane organizations in the country were making a case to the judicial authorities who would decide the dogs' fate that they were, as a group, too "far gone" to be saved, and that "euthanizing" them was the kindest thing to do for them, and the best thing to do for society at large. On the other side stood Best Friends and other rescue organizations committed to putting a no-kill philosophy into practical effect by reaching out to as many of these dogs as possible and offering them a second chance. Although they were all committed to bringing an end to dog fighting, puppy mills, and other instances of animal cruelty, Best Friends and those other national organizations saw this issue from completely different perspectives. As Best Friends president Michael Mountain put it, "With a group of dogs rescued from the deep trauma of sadism and murder, destroying them is not an option. So, rehabilitation, healing, and redemption have to take its place…. It's only when you take killing off the table as a way of 'helping' the animals that you really start looking for new ways that are truly going to work."

In December, the ruling came down: the 47 surviving pit bulls would be placed with several different sanctuary organizations, and 22 of them who needed the most special care would go to Best Friends. Less than a month later, Best Friends' 22 arrived at Dogtown: among them were Lucas and Curly and Tug and Halle and Shadow and Willy and Ray and Bonita and Little Red and Handsome Dan. Since the court decision, staff at the sanctuary in Utah had been working hard to retrofit one of the octagons at Dogtown so that each of the Vick dogs—now dubbed Vicktory Dogs by the Best Friends folk—would have his or her own play area as well as indoor space. All was ready when the vans and trucks pulled in to Dogtown on January 2, 2008. Lots of tails were wagging as the travel crates were unloaded, but there were many of the group who were clearly still terrified, and reticent of any human contact.

Little Red was one of those in particularly poor shape. She had permanent scars on her face and her teeth had been filed down, a likely indication that she had been used as a kind of sparring partner for the main fighters, a "bait" dog for them to literally sharpen their skills on. She was shivering with fear when they all arrived and stayed as far from humans as she could.

LUCAS wears the battle scars from his time as a champion fighter for Bad Newz Kennels, Michael Vick's infamous dogfighting ring. His greatest triumph, though, was being selected as one of the 22 rescued pit bulls to come to the Best Friends sanctuary. Like most of the other Vicktory Dogs, he has proved exceptionally affectionate and eager to please—he jumps up on the doghouse in his play area whenever visitors come by so no one will miss him and greets his caregivers with tail-wagging and kisses.

LITTLE RED beds down with Ed Fritz, one of Dogtown's managers, in her play area. Initially terrified of people, Little Red had limited contact with caregivers at first, then learned to get used to Ed. Later, she was introduced to other members of the Best Friends staff, but only when she was comfortable enough. Patience worked wonders in her case; she now enjoys greeting visitors.

Many of the dogs required physical healing, something the Best Friends medical staff was well prepared to handle. But the emotional and psychological wounds these dogs bore were a different matter. Many of them were showing signs of psychological injury that in certain ways resembled post-traumatic stress disorder, the psychological condition that affects some soldiers and victims of warfare and other traumatic events. "Some hard-nosed scientists remain unconvinced that animals have emotions," says Best Friends vet Dr. Frank McMillan, "but animals with emotional scars act in much the same way as traumatized humans. You can tell they are struggling." Part of the issue for many of the dogs was that they may have been forced to endure abusive training; one standard technique in training dogs for fighting is to beat them severely, then reward them with food so that they learn to tolerate pain.

One of the big challenges for the caregivers was not knowing exactly what each specific dog had been through—important information that could potentially provide valuable guidance in their rehabilitation. But there were significant clues. Dr. Frank surmised, for example, that a dog who shied away from people altogether was probably poorly socialized as a puppy and denied pleasant and positive interactions with humans. Dogs who would come toward a person, then suddenly cower or shy away, were more likely to have been psychologically abused and physically beaten.

LITTLE RED

But there were still lots of questions: had a given dog been beaten or otherwise abused, or had he or she been subjected to stamina training on a treadmill to the point of exhaustion? Had food been a reward for viciousness or an enticement to endure pain? Had a breeding female been confined for a few weeks or for years?

Given the circumstances, the answers would likely never emerge. With best guesses, though, the vets and caregivers would move forward to help the Vicktory Dogs take the first steps toward recovery. And the caregivers would also surround them with the compassion they couldn't help but feel for these abused creatures. It was perhaps the best medicine of all.

Number one on Dr. Frank's list of approaches was finding every way possible to reduce the level of stress in the dogs' present lives. Initially, caregivers spent a fair amount of time just observing the dogs and noting whatever it was that seemed to cause them any degree of distress. "Once we know what

HALLE, one of the Vicktory Dogs, strains away from caregiver Keith while Dr. Frank, clipboard in hand, evaluates her behavior. All the dogs were routinely rated on a scale of 1 to 10 in such categories as fear, interest in toys, and overall socialization skills. Halle, who had likely been used for breeding rather than fighting, was exceptionally anxious when she first arrived at Dogtown and fearful of people—breeding dogs typically experienced little or no human contact. She soon benefited from therapeutic massage and other techniques designed to ease her stress.

is emotionally upsetting," Dr. Frank says, "we can work to minimize the psychological impact of the distressful stimuli." It's an approach used in treating people with post-traumatic stress as well and is initially valuable for creating a relative calmness so that further healing can begin. But Dr. Frank also had to deal with generalized anxiety in these dogs, and he had a couple of medicinal approaches in his arsenal.

One was the use of a dog-appeasing pheromone, or DAP. "It's a pheromone that mother dogs secrete around their breast glands to ease their puppies' anxiety," Dr. Frank explains, and it's available as a spray that can be dispensed from a wall diffuser or even incorporated into a collar. The caregiving teams also employed proven natural anti-anxiety aromatherapy treatments, including lavender and chamomile essence. "They don't all work on every individual, so you have to experiment with different ones on different animals," Dr. Frank says. "But when aromatherapy works, it's so nice."

Then, of course, there was the classic Best Friends technique of gentle approaches, incremental handling, and patience, patience, patience. One of the simple secrets of success is that there is no clock ticking on any of the animals. Time is not of the essence. And perhaps the most important thing of all was the unlimited, round-the-clock love the caregivers were showing the dogs. There was, after all, a world of cruelty and abuse to make up for. Everyone who worked with the Vick dogs felt their hearts going out to them.

Some of the dogs made fairly rapid steps forward. Ed Fritz, one of the managers of Dogtown, helped some of the more people-oriented ones by sleeping with them in their play areas. Little Red, the presumed bait dog, made major progress after spending nights curled up next to Ed. Other, more fearful ones had to be handled slow step by slow step. They would get a chance to know a few caregivers who would be their main contact, and who would work daily to get them used to a close human presence, with no actual handling and minimal interaction. As animal care adviser Jeff Popowich puts it, "The basis of anything you do with animals is building a trusting relationship. Then you can challenge them and expose them to different situations. It's like convincing a kid to go to the dentist." Later, such dogs would be introduced to another new person, and the patient socialization process would sometimes begin all over again.

Tug gets a hug from Michael Hand, and Willie gets similar loving from another of the Vicktory Dog caregivers. Willie was at first terrified of crossing any threshold at his new home in Dogtown's Pittie City, perhaps remembering what had happened to him whenever he was brought from the kennels at Michael Vick's property into a dogfighting ring. Patient work has helped him past that fear, and he now enjoys playing with toys—chief among them his food dish. Tug got his name because of his eagerness on walks. He, too, has overcome his initial fear of loud noises and camera flashes.

43

TUG

WILLIE

SHADOW

Observation remained crucial. Based on Dr. Frank's instructions, caregivers evaluated every dog on a daily basis, scoring them from 1 to 10 on such factors as confidence, fear, energy level, positive interest in and affection for people, interest in toys and other personal enrichments, and overall enjoyment of life. Progress on the scale was a very effective guide to what was working.

At their own different rates, virtually all the Vicktory Dogs advanced in their rehabilitation. The process is ongoing, but Dr. Frank and other staffers are confident that most of them will eventually be able to be adopted into carefully chosen homes. Meanwhile the caregiving teams relished the individual successes — signs that all the loving and compassion was having a positive, healing effect.

Shadow's story will tug at the heartstrings of just about every dog owner who knows well the exuberance that erupts when the leash comes out. Shadow was petrified of the leash, almost more so than he was afraid of people, cowering in the farthest corner of his crate. Whenever he saw a leash he would wince as if expecting to be hit. Caregivers worked very slowly with him, starting by leaving the leash on the ground so he could sniff at it and learn that it wasn't going to do him any harm. After a while, they hooked the leash to his collar and let him drag it around, then when he seemed comfortable they would take him for miniature walks around his own enclosed area. Finally, with encouragement from treats and praise and lots of petting, he started going on real walks with a staff member along some of Dogtown's many pathways. Now Shadow responds like just about every well-loved, well-cared-for dog: the leash comes out, and he's eager to get going.

And then there's Handsome Dan, a big solid pit bull who had somehow weathered his Bad Newz days. In addition to having that same fear of leashes, he was afraid to go through doorways or over thresholds. Caregivers used much the same tactics with him that had worked with Shadow, a slow habituation to what was frightening him, and soon he was making similar progress. But his handlers noticed one thing they weren't initially sure how to address: Dan was now so full of energy on his eagerly awaited walks that he would sometimes pull walkers right off their feet. The Dogtown solution? Patience was again the watchword. Although ultimately the Best Friends trainers will want him to walk normally on the leash, the first goal was to get him the therapeutic exercise he so obviously craved. Handsome Dan was one of the first Vicktory Dogs to get to try a new technique: being harnessed to a fat-wheeled scooter that can handle the bumpy terrain of Dogtown paths. Handsome Dan was hesitant at first, as he had been about anything new, and he still isn't too sure of doorways or thrilled to be harnessed up. But when he got out with that scooter and didn't have to worry about the pull of a human to hold him back, he was off to the races, his scooter-mounted caregiver flying beside him, along for the ride.

The stories go on and on, just about every one of them with its own triumphs. The ironic thing about the Vicktory Dogs is that their eagerness to please was to some extent what got them involved in dogfighting to begin with: because pit bulls are so devoted to humans, they will do just about anything that's asked of

HANDSOME DAN

HANDSOME DAN takes caregiver Bill for a ride on a scooter specially designed to handle Dogtown's rough trails. Although Handsome Dan and other brimming-with-energy Vicktory Dogs are eventually taught good leash behavior, the goal at first is to get them a form of exercise they may never have experienced before. Many dogfighting dogs are force-exercised on treadmills, typically to the point of exhaustion. Freedom to run is a newfound pleasure.

them. The work of Best Friends is to reconvince these inherently loyal creatures that good will come of their devotion. And the surest way to show that was in the simple fact of the devotion their caregivers were giving them, from the most genuine places in their own hearts.

Out of the Flood: The Katrina Rescue

Trauma comes in many different forms. Late in the summer of 2005 in New Orleans and the surrounding Gulf Coast region, it came in the form of the worst hurricane to hit the U.S. mainland in decades. Katrina rolled into New Orleans over the weekend, and at first officials and citizens alike were encouraged that the city appeared to have weathered the storm. But the protective levees had been fatally weakened and soon breached; by Monday the city was filling with water, and its inhabitants were evacuating in droves—the vast majority without their beloved pets, whom evacuees had been told to leave behind.

As soon as he heard the news, Paul Berry, executive director of Best Friends and a native of New Orleans, headed to the area, arriving the day after the storm hit. He began organizing a temporary rescue center at the St. Francis Animal Sanctuary in Tylertown, Mississippi, about 100 miles north of New Orleans.

A team of rescuers from Best Friends arrived a few days later, having driven from Utah with all the supplies

Stranded on the hood of a submerged car for perhaps as long as two weeks, this Rottweiler mix was sick—most likely from drinking polluted water—and emaciated when she was first rescued. Katrina dogs were ferried to Tylertown, Mississippi, 100 miles north of New Orleans, for medical evaluation and emergency care. Rescuers always noted where dogs had been found, entering the information in a database in the hopes of being able to reunite dogs with their families.

47

An improvised "bucket brigade" unloads supplies at Tylertown. Pet food, bedding, and other necessary items arrived by the truckload almost hourly, donated by Best Friends members and other sponsors. Those responsible for organizing efforts at Tylertown rarely had to tell volunteers what to do; everyone pitched in where the need was greatest.

they could think of—generators, food, collars and leashes and catchpoles, crates, medical supplies, fencing material, tarpaulins for sun protection, twist ties, duct tape, and so on. It was an amazingly prescient list, as almost everything came in handy. Looking back, the only thing they would have done differently was not bring food: once word of the rescue operation got out through the Best Friends network, half a ton of food was arriving by truck and van almost every hour, donated by supporters from around the country.

After a brief layover in Tylertown, rescue teams headed to the city, bucking a steady stream of evacuees going in the opposite direction. Paul used all his skills of persuasion to get through military roadblocks and obtain permission to go searching for abandoned pets in the flooded streets. He also arranged to procure johnboats for the teams because it was the only way to get around. One volunteer drove back home to Alabama to get his own boat, which he donated to the cause; it was a 600-mile round trip, and he did it overnight.

All day, day after day, the rescuers saved pets—cats, birds, small animals, but mostly dogs, dogs, and more dogs. They found them in attics, in unflooded alleys, in abandoned boats, and time and again perched precariously on car rooftops, doing all they could to stay out of the water. Many of the dogs were pit bulls—dogfighting groups had proliferated in the city. Because of their devotion to people, the pits turned out to be among the easiest dogs to rescue; they would sometimes even swim out to meet an approaching rescue boat. But Paul remembers one particularly chilling situation: four pit bulls chained at the top of a flight of outdoor stairs on the side of a decrepit building. Two of them were tied almost face to face, and the stronger was attacking the slighter one, with occasional help from the other two. Paul first heard the horrific sound of them fighting, the weaker one sometimes yelping in pain, from blocks away.

He got to the stairs and walked up slowly, careful not to make eye contact, which can ramp up an aggressive dog. "I got to the very top step where they could get to me if they wanted to, and they were growling and all that stuff, and I just sat down with my back to them and started talking to them, telling them calmly that I was going to get them some water, get them some food, get the chains off them and get them into the boat." Then he carefully reached back, got his

Jeff Popowich hoists a pit bull aboard one of Best Friends' rescue boats. She was in bad shape and needed immediate care at the off-loading spot beyond the floodwaters; IV fluids revived her. "She was nervous when we got her—we were strangers, after all," Jeff recalls. "But as soon as I picked her up, she just melted in my arms."

hand between the two who had been fighting, and managed to get first one, then each of them in turn, off their chains. "As soon as I got the chains off their necks, they would just fall into me, into my chest. They'd let me hold them, and as they put their head on my shoulder, I could just tell they were thinking, 'Thank God a human's here to help me.'"

The rescue teams kept detailed records of where dogs were found, logging them into a database that was later posted on the Internet. As a result, hundreds of dogs made their way back to their overjoyed owners. In one case, a team driving back to Tylertown noticed that one dog still had his tags on, and there was a phone number. They called the number. A woman picked up the phone, and they described the dog to her. She gasped, and then they heard her turn away from the phone and scream, "They found Buddy! They found Buddy!" She and her family were at an evacuation site—the number was for her cell phone. The Best Friends rescuer told her that Buddy would be at Tylertown being taken care of. There was a moment of silence, and then they heard her shout Buddy's name once again with joy.

Rescues continued for weeks, even after the floodwaters receded. As many as 70 dogs were arriving at Tylertown a day, and volunteers had constructed runs to house more than 600 dogs at a time. All of them got medical evaluations and necessary care, grooming, and as much attention as the busy rescuers could spare.

The payoff was those reunions. Every time someone came to pick up their pet at Tylertown, a volunteer would get an old pot and beat on it with a spoon, ringing a joyous note that lifted everyone's spirits. But even most of those dogs not reunited with their families found good new homes. Some of them came to Dogtown for further recuperation or special care. Tylertown kept

Jeff cuddles a little black ball of fur in Tylertown. Puppies such as this one were rescued from abandoned shelters, the top floors of flooded homes, and locations that had obviously been backyard breeding operations. "There was a lot of sadness and some bad memories of what we saw in New Orleans," Jeff says, "but to me it's just amazing that a bunch of people went down there and saved all those dogs."

This happy little hound mix waits in Tylertown with other rescued dogs for the next step on his road to a new life. He had been tethered in the back of an abandoned pickup truck, his cries attracting the attention of the rescue team, who had already brought the johnboat out of the water at the end of a long day; they relaunched the boat and headed back to save him. By the time the Tylertown sanctuary closed up shop eight months after the hurricane, all the rescued dogs had either been reunited with their people, placed in new homes, or brought back to Dogtown for special care.

the good work up for more than eight months—so much for its being a temporary shelter. And because of the efforts of Best Friends and other rescue organizations, government policy was changed: in the future, evacuees would be allowed to take their pets with them.

War's Invisible Victims: The Beirut Rescue

Dogs from far away are sometimes flown into the Kanab airport only a few short miles from the sanctuary. Travel crates with water bottles attached (bottom) keep dogs comfortable during transport.

52

After the experience of Katrina, Best Friends turned what had been a well-organized but impromptu effort into an established arm of the sanctuary's outreach efforts, forming so-called Rapid Response teams to address similar circumstances that might occur in the future. It wasn't long before these "official" teams got a chance to show their stuff.

In the summer of 2006, fighting broke out between Israel and the Hezbollah in Lebanon. As always in war, it's catastrophic not only for innocent civilians, but for the animals who are caught in the crossfire and abandoned as whole populations flee their homes and villages. The worst suffering was to animals in southern Lebanon, where the entire region was in turmoil. And while you can often find dozens of humane groups in a single American or European town, Lebanon had but one small humane society. Beirut for the Ethical Treatment of Animals, or BETA (no relation to the American group PETA), was doing its best to rescue and shelter as many injured strays, including farm animals, as possible, as well as feeding starving animals at small zoos, but the staff, numbering simply 12 volunteers, was completely overwhelmed. Their three shelters in Beirut had all been shattered in the bombing and they'd moved all the dogs and cats to temporary refuges outside the city.

As soon as the airport reopened, Best Friends sent in a team and began organizing its first international rescue effort. Arrangements began in Utah to gather supplies—crates, food, medical supplies—and ship them to Lebanon. The Best Friends flight, with vets and other volunteers aboard, was one of the first planes to get into Lebanon after Israel lifted its air blockade.

After assessing the situation on the ground, the Best Friends Rapid Response team decided the best way to help the BETA volunteers rebuild their humane society and begin to focus on spay/neuter and adoption programs was to lift the burden of caring for the dogs and cats from the shelters that had been destroyed. Many of the animals had been injured, and a plan was quickly hatched to fly them back to Best Friends Animal Sanctuary. Back in Utah, temporary shelters were set up in one of the horse pastures, with fencing, tents, play areas, and the like—much of it the very same material that had been used in Tylertown. Dogtown was, in effect, expanded to include this new annex. Then, in September, after a trip that took 48 hours altogether, 150 dogs and 145 cats arrived at the sanctuary.

ANDREA and her new forever person, Susan, begin the bonding process at Dogtown shortly after Susan adopted her. Many of the Lebanese dogs were in fairly good shape despite the trauma of their circumstances and readily found new homes; others had broken bones, shrapnel wounds, and other medical problems that required treatment at the Dogtown clinic. Susan gave Andrea a new name, Aneksi, an Egyptian word meaning "She belongs to me."

53

SCHTROUMPFETTE, one of the Beirut dogs, was shivering with fear when she arrived at the Dogtown annex known as Little Lebanon. Sherry Woodard, Best Friends' chief animal behaviorist, got in her large crate with her and began speaking softly, only slowly reaching out to pet her. Within an hour, Schtroumpfette was settled enough to let Sherry hold her. Schtroumpfette's rehabilitation was slow at first, and Sherry was about the only person who could get close. But the renowned Best Friends patience eventually paid off. Six months after her rescue, Schtroumpfette was secure and socialized enough to go to an adoption event in Arizona. Her travel crate came back empty—she had been adopted.

54

Amazingly, most of the dogs were in fairly decent shape and seemed remarkably resilient, ready to play as soon as they got out of their carrying crates. It's likely that many of these were house pets who had been decently cared for. But there were also many who were traumatized and would need extra attention. One of these was a beautiful mixed pointer named Schtroumpfette—French for "Smurfette." No one knew the specifics of her circumstances, even who had given her the somewhat quirky name. But as soon as she saw her, Sherry Woodard, Best Friends' resident behavioral expert, knew she needed help. She wouldn't come out of her crate and was just shaking. "So I went into the crate with her," Sherry recalls, and she began to comfort the frightened dog. Only when Schtroumpfette was ready, after 20 or so minutes, did Sherry lead her out of the crate to her new temporary home in the Dogtown annex.

Over the next weeks, Sherry and Schtroumpfette formed a relationship. Sherry would feed her by hand to help ease her anxiety with people, and slowly introduced her to "strangers" in the form of other staff members and volunteers. "She had some skill with other dogs but she was fearful there as well," Sherry says, so she adopted the same approach of cautious, slow introductions and brief times spent together with other dogs.

Slowly through the fall and winter, Schtroumpfette made steady progress. She was a beautiful dog, and once Sherry judged that she had recovered from her traumatic time back in Lebanon, she was sent out on an adoption event in Arizona. Sherry stayed back at Dogtown and was thrilled to hear when the Best Friends team returned that Schtroumpfette and 32 other dogs from the Lebanon rescue were now in their forever homes.

Another lucky dog was a shepherd mix named Jazz. He was one of the first Lebanese dogs to be adopted, by a woman named

55

Terese from New Jersey. Jazz adjusted fairly well to his new home and was soon trotting around the house carrying one of his favorite objects, a five-pound exercise weight. But Terese felt something wasn't entirely right. For one thing, Jazz wasn't bonding with her other dog, Misty.

Terese thought she knew what the problem was. Jazz had been brought from Lebanon together with another dog, named Flower. Records indicated they had lived together before, so when they moved into Dogtown, they were allowed to stay together. They were both such good-natured dogs that staffers didn't think it would be a problem if they got adopted separately, and that's how Terese got Jazz.

A year and a half later, bothered about the little adjustment issues, Terese happened to notice a dog named Flower on the Best Friends website. Sure enough, it was Jazz's old pal, still waiting to be adopted. It didn't take Terese long to decide she had room for one more dog at home, and soon Flower was on her way to New Jersey as well. When the two dogs met, it was almost as if they didn't know each other; Terese said it was like two old friends barely recognizing each other at a high school reunion. But within days, it was clear they had reconnected. The three dogs now make a happy family. Flower follows Jazz around wherever he goes, almost as if she's still learning the ropes of her new home—or at least she wants Jazz to think that.

FLOWER

56

A DOG'S BEST FRIEND

Vet on a Mission

Patti Iampietro turned her passion for animals into a profession, graduating from veterinary school in 1993. She specialized in emergency medicine and surgery, as well as volunteering at shelters. After Hurricane Katrina she went down to New Orleans to assist with relief efforts, and that's where she first heard about Best Friends. The combination of her experiences in the Gulf Coast region and what she'd learned about Best Friends led her to become one of the sanctuary's three staff veterinarians.

Dr. Patti has been involved with several of Best Friends' recent major rescue missions. She was at the airport at midnight when all the dogs arrived from Lebanon in 2006 and immediately started medical evaluations. Many of them had bad fractures, missing legs, scars, and other wounds that had to be attended to. And although they had all been given rigorous health checks before entering the country, the dogs from Beirut were kept in a part of the sanctuary separate from Dogtown for six weeks. Part of Dr. Patti's routine—after finishing regular rounds in Dogtown—was to head down to "Little Lebanon" to continue their care. It was exhausting but satisfying work.

She also helped with many of the Vicktory Dogs from the infamous dogfighting ring. "Working with them is a benefit to me," Dr. Patti comments. "These dogs have had so much hardship, stress, and trauma, and I think it stays with them. It's a gift to me to be able to help them." She took special pleasure in working with Animal/Noble and Gonzo, two of the dogs rescued from a puppy mill in Nebraska. She ministered to their medical needs but also helped with their psychological rehabilitation, and like so many caregivers at Dogtown felt she was reaping rewards in the process: "They give us something, and we give them something. It's amazing how kindness and patience can turn a dog around."

Whether it's a war-traumatized dog, a puppy who has never known love, or a big, adorable hunk like Gavin (above), who somehow survived for 35 days on his own in and around Las Vegas scrounging for food, Dr. Patti gives them all her utmost, as much for herself as for them. "Working at Best Friends, my life as a veterinarian is dedicated to making the world of these animals better. Since coming here I've been given the opportunity to help so many more animals and to be a part of what Best Friends stands for. There's nothing better than knowing that I'm a part of that."

57

58

Caregiver Tamara and Tobin spend a last few affectionate moments together before Tobin leaves for his new forever home (far right). So strong is the bond between humans and canines at Dogtown that mixed emotions often accompany the happy event of adoption. Kunzite (above) routinely won hearts during her six months at New Friends, and Mills (inset) seems to be competing for biggest smile with volunteer Warren.

The Best Place to Be

How Dogtown Changes Lives

Temporary shelter or permanent safe haven, the first good home they've ever known or a return to a loving environment they'd lost, Dogtown is there to be whatever its inhabitants need. After getting the special care they require, most of the dogs at the sanctuary are soon ready to be placed in good new homes. But for some of them, Dogtown itself will be their forever home, and with all the love and companionship they receive there, it's as good a home as they could ever have imagined.

WILLA reaches up for her morning meatball (above). Caregiver Ann prepares to take several dogs for their morning walk (right).

Meatballs for Breakfast

Michelle Logan, one of several dozen caregivers who work at Dogtown on any given day, starts the morning at Conrad and Leopold's making meatballs. She has 32 dogs to feed in the two octagons, and each and every one of them gets a meatball before breakfast. Michelle opens the cans of food appropriate for each dog's assigned diet—some have low-calorie requirements, others hypoallergenic food and so on—and she scoops out a spoonful to make the meatball. She's not just being nice to the dogs in her care; there's a serious purpose to the treat. One of the dogs in her group, Fred, has intestinal problems and needs medication about 20 minutes before he eats. Michelle tucks it into the meatball, and because he lives with three or four other dogs in his run, everybody

gets one so no one will feel left out. There's another reason as well. "We noticed the other day that Bandit's face looked a little swollen," Michelle says, referring to another of her charges who had developed an infection. "If he wasn't used to getting a meatball, it might be a little tricky getting him to take the antibiotic he needs. But because he always knows a meatball is coming, I can just slip the pill right in."

It's the kind of specialized care that sets Best Friends apart. Every caregiver is familiar with every dog in his or her charge, and part of the daily routine is checking on all of them, first thing. "I always take a look around when I arrive in the morning," Michelle says, "to make sure everybody's doing okay." Then her chores begin. After dishing out food—and, as necessary, tethering dogs who might be tempted to nose in on one of their friends' chow— she gathers up any bedding that needs to be washed, does a little poop-scooping, and checks on the availability of volunteers to help with walking, which takes up the rest of the morning. Walks are pleasure time for caregivers and canines alike, a chance to do a little training but mostly just a time to enjoy companionship.

Staffers prepare individually tailored meals for all the dogs in their care; medications are included in plastic bags and will be inserted into wet-food meatball treats. Each pair of octagons in Dogtown Heights has its own kitchen area.

Spotlight on: Grover

Toward the end of the morning, Michelle often takes a couple of dogs to Dogtown's two-acre dog park to spend some time in a different environment while staff members have lunch. It was something she always enjoyed doing with Grover, a Labrador retriever mix she became quite fond of, and his best friend, Tinkerbell. Grover had "issues," as they say. He'd been found tied to a tree in Seal Beach, California, and rescued by the local shelter. He'd even been adopted, but it hadn't worked out. He had terrible separation anxiety and had torn up the inside of his person's car when left alone one time. He was also terrified of thunderstorms, quivering with stress at every rumble. Through connections, he'd ended up at Best Friends, where the vets prescribed a tranquilizer that helped tremendously, both with his fear of thunderstorms and his separation anxiety. He also got regular sessions in the hydrotherapy tank, which helped with a bad shoulder that sometimes caused him to limp.

There was one other issue with Grover, though: he was a "jumper." A few Dogtown residents have the same problem, clambering up chainlink fences and making their way out. Grover lived in a so-called jump run, whose fencing is topped with a horizontal piece of additional fencing to prevent occupants from climbing over. It wasn't that Grover wanted to escape and run away; he just never liked to be without human companionship. Usually he was okay when Tinkerbell was around, so one day Michelle decided to leave the two of them alone in the dog park, which has normal fencing. She headed back to the clinic to have lunch with some friends. A short time later, Grover came trotting down the path, happily wagging his tail when he caught sight of Michelle. Another time, as his anxiety seemed to be waning, she'd tried keeping him in a different run that had very high fencing but that wasn't topped off. He seemed okay, and Michelle was sure the fencing was too high for him even if he tried to get out. She left him there for the night, hoping this would demonstrate some progress that might make Grover a better candidate for adoption. The next morning when the first staff member arrived, there was Grover in the parking lot, just hanging out and waiting for somebody to show up.

Grover lived in Dogtown for more than seven years. He

GROVER Climber extraordinaire, Grover could get over just about any fence that wasn't specially designed to keep "jumpers" in. But Grover was never really escaping: he just couldn't stand being without human companionship and was always trying to find where the people were. His separation anxiety, which was sometimes destructive, made him a tough case for adoption, but his Dogtown caregivers never gave up. After more than seven years at the Best Friends sanctuary, Grover was adopted by Steven and Patricia, a retired couple who could meet his needs.

Michelle Besmehn comforts Tuffy shortly after he was found severely wounded at an abandoned shelter in Nevada (top). Tuffy was in shock and dangerously close to death in the first few hours; his listlessness during transport (above) greatly concerned his rescuers. His condition was so extreme that the vets couldn't risk sedating him to clean his wounds thoroughly.

seemed on his way to being a permanent resident, but he was such a sweet dog, with so many great qualities, that volunteers and staffers kept holding out hope that he'd find a forever family of his own. Finally, in the spring of 2008, the right family found him. Patricia and Steven had read Grover's story in the special needs section of *Best Friends* magazine and felt drawn to him. They were a retired couple and assured the Best Friends home evaluators that Grover would have constant companionship. They even made arrangements to buy a new car that was lower to the ground so Grover, who was getting on by this point (his jumping days behind him), would have no trouble getting in and out. It was a sign of the degree of their commitment. A few weeks later, Michelle watched with mixed emotions as her dear old friend headed off with his new family.

Spotlight on: Tuffy

"Never Give Up" could be the slogan of Dogtown. Sometimes, as in a case like Grover's, it applies to the seemingly infinite patience of Best Friends' staffers as they hang in there year after year, doing the best they can for special needs cases, ever optimistic that it's just a matter of time before the right match comes along. Indeed, that patience is what sets Best Friends apart from many other well-intentioned shelters that feel they have to give up on dogs with difficult health or behavioral problems to focus their energies and resources on those more likely to be adopted. Best Friends looks at things another way: giving up on any animal is simply not an option, so whatever it takes is precisely what Best Friends provides.

Sometimes, though, never giving up has more to do with the perseverance and resilience that lies at the core of almost every dog. In those cases, Best Friends sees its task as giving that life force an opportunity to express itself. There may be no better instance of that than the story of Tuffy.

Tuffy—a name his rescuers gave him—was discovered near death in the Nevada desert at an abandoned, overrun shelter whose owner had died. Tuffy had crawled to the flimsy protection of a hay bale after being attacked by roaming wild dogs and possibly other wild animals. His wounds included two deep bites and a horrific injury along his right side, which was torn away down to the muscle, coated in filth and clearly infected. Michelle Besmehn,

TUFFY was transformed after adoption by the Steele family. He and Hunter, the Steeles' youngest, quickly formed a special bond.

TUFFY

TUFFY joins the Steeles and their three other dogs for a family portrait. "We can't imagine what life would be like without him," mother Jodie says.

who is Dogtown's manager and was part of the Rapid Response team that had gone to the rescue, cradled Tuffy's head in her lap shortly after he was found. "I put my hand under his chin and he looked up at me and relaxed his head," she remembers. "I think he knew help had arrived."

Tuffy was crated for transport to the nearest vet's office, more than two hours away. Animal care adviser Jeff Popowich noticed that his gums were almost white, indicating that he was in shock. "I knew he was close to dying," Jeff recalls. "I seriously think if we hadn't found him that day, he would have died that night." He got emergency treatment with IV antibiotics and some pain medication, but he was too fragile to sedate, so they could only do minimal wound cleaning.

The Best Friends team flew Tuffy back to the clinic at Dogtown the next day in their four-seater rescue plane, and intensive medical treatment began. He still seemed too weak for sedation, so the vets and vet techs focused their efforts on keeping his wounds clean as best they could and giving him antibiotics. The next day, much to everyone's surprise, Tuffy was standing on his own and wagging his tail. A day later, the vets decided he could tolerate sedation, so he underwent deep surgical cleaning. After that, the wounds were cleaned thoroughly every day until it was clear he'd fought off the infections. There was still a lot of healing left for him to do, but Tuffy—who spent every night at home with Jeff and his family, including dogs—was on his way to recovering.

After barely a month at Dogtown, Tuffy was adopted by the Steeles, who already had three other dogs, four children, cockatiels, and a turtle at home. Tuffy made progress recuperating, and soon hair was growing back over healthy pink skin along his side. He was also getting more comfortable trusting the other dogs and not being possessive over food. Soon his true puppy nature was front and center, and just about anything shreddable—including three shower curtains—paid the price. "Is Tuffy work?" Jodie Steele, the mom, asks rhetorically. "Yes. Is he worth it? Absolutely. We can't imagine what life would be like without him."

Many people tell the Steeles how lucky Tuffy was to land with such a caring family. "We are the ones who are blessed," replies Jodie. "Tuffy brings much joy to our family."

Spotlight on: Kunzite

Another Dogtown denizen with apparently more than her fair share of endurance is Kunzite, named for a stunningly beautiful natural crystal, a tribute to this strong-willed dog's striking appearance. Kunzite has one blue and one grayish brown eye in a black-and-white face, and her two pointy ears seem almost always on alert. She has looked the picture of perfect health since day one at Dogtown, but in this case looks were potentially deceiving. Kunzite was born at New Friends, the building reserved for puppies, her mother a mixed Border collie/heeler named Amber who had been in a nearby shelter that

KUNZITE gets a mouthful of one of her stuffed animals (above), who didn't last long, chewing being one of Kunzie's favorite pastimes.

didn't have room for a dog about to have puppies. Nine little bundles of fur were born that day in December of 2006, and everything seemed fine until two days later, when Amber began vomiting and having diarrhea. The vets tested her and discovered she had parvovirus, which would threaten her pups' lives if she wasn't isolated from them right away. The nine puppies were divvied up among three foster families—all Best Friends staff—to be bottle-fed and cared for virtually on an hourly basis. Amber was successfully treated for the virus and was eventually adopted.

Puppies as young as these can do nothing for themselves, so the foster families had to do everything, right down to holding a warm wet washcloth on them to help them urinate—simulating what their mother would have done by licking them. It was far from the best circumstance for newborns, and everyone involved was concerned. Kunzite seemed to be doing all right, but unfortunately the two other pups with her died at the end of the first week. In the next four or five weeks, the others began dying as well. The vets determined that the pups had caught the virus while still in the womb, and it was affecting their hearts and lungs; they were literally outgrowing these vital organs.

By the sixth week, Kunzite and one other sibling, Ellie Mae, were the only ones left. There was an unavoidable air of gloom among those who had done the fostering, but Kunzite's foster mother, a Dogtown trainer named Dara, not sure how long Kunzite herself would last, was determined to give her the best life possible for whatever time she had left. She kept up the rigorous bottle-feeding schedule, getting up two or three times during the night, and also spent lots of time interacting with Kunzie—her new nickname—to make up for the fact that she had lost the valuable socialization experience of being with her mother and littermates.

Kunzie couldn't be introduced to other dogs or puppies because her immune system was too vulnerable.

As the weeks rolled by, Kunzite continued to progress, moving from the bottle to a nutrient-rich gruel and ultimately to dry food. She was using her puppy pee pads—a more absorbent form of the old standard newspaper—almost without accident and was even starting to ask to be let out when she needed to. Dara was also impressed with how readily she was picking up on the basic command of "sit." Dara used a strategy she had previously found effective—demonstrating the action by gently moving Kunzite into a sit position, repeating this several times, and only including the verbal command when Kunzie was good at the

KUNZITE was a cuddly bundle right from the start. Here she enjoys some lap time with her foster parents, Best Friends staffers Danielle and Ross.

action. As Dara explains, this meant Kunzite was only having to learn one thing at a time.

Kunzite was doing well, she had gotten all her necessary vaccinations, and soon she was able to interact with other puppies at Tara's Run, picking up essential canine socialization skills every time. She was a bundle of energy and showed a particular knack with many of the obstacles in the agility course—a sign of her Border collie heritage. But at the beginning of April, sad news came for all those who had been involved with Amber's puppies. Ellie Mae, who had been adopted by a Dogtown staff member, was brought to the Dogtown clinic because her breathing had become shallow and rapid. Tests showed she had an enlarged, weakened heart, and despite the medical team's best efforts, Ellie Mae died a few days later.

The team decided they'd have to check on Kunzite as well, and she got a complete set of tests. X-rays showed that her heart was slightly enlarged but all her vital signs were strong. She was now being fostered by Best Friends staffers Danielle and Ross. They were of course concerned but decided not to pamper her in any way, letting her live as fully as she clearly wanted to. She made visits to Danielle's office, went for car rides into town, and even joined Ross at a biker rally. She was growing by leaps and bounds, her legs lengthening, and despite entering that somewhat clumsy phase of puppyhood, she continued to charm everyone who met her. She was a particularly big hit with the bikers.

By this time, Kunzite was well known among Best Friends members. Her story was being updated regularly on the Guardian Angel section of the website, where members can read about some of the animals receiving special care at the sanctuary and donate to help them, and several families had offered to adopt her. But her

KUNZITE AND JASPER concentrate on an anticipated treat (left). Kunzie's forever family also includes Miles, Pamela, and Lizzy (center, above). Jasper wasn't too sure about Kunzie at first but he soon came around—though he seemed reluctant to admit it. "I caught them playing outside together a couple of times," Pamela says, "but as soon as Jasper would see me, he'd stop as if to say, 'I don't like this new dog, really.'"

71

foster family wanted to be sure she went to the right place, to a family who understood the risks and would be willing to hang in there no matter what. In the beginning of May, that family emerged, a couple named Pamela and Miles who had two Border collies and thus knew intimately how much energy these dogs have and need to expend to be truly happy. One line in their application struck home: "We want the chance to give her a good home regardless of how long or short her life may be." As Ross and Danielle wrote in Kunzite's online journal, "There are times in life when something just feels right, and this was definitely one of those times."

Kunzite met her new family and everything went well. She joined her forever home in May and began the life everyone involved in her care felt she deserved. "When we first adopted Kunzite eight months ago," Pam wrote in Kunzite's online journal shortly after her first birthday, "we did so with the knowledge that she may not be a part of our lives for very long . . . but something inside told me she was meant to be ours, and I haven't looked back since. It really is hard to have a bad day with her around, living each day to the fullest, taking in everything she possibly can, as we all should."

The Tragedy of Puppy Mills

Kunzite didn't get the best start in life, but for tens of thousands of puppies things are even worse. The numbers vary, but animal welfare organizations estimate that somewhere between 4,000 and 5,000 so-called puppy mills exist in the United States, a few of which have as many as 1,000 breeding dogs. Multiply that by typical litter sizes and you get a sense of how many dogs are subjected to the horrific living conditions that prevail at the vast majority of these mass production dog-breeding facilities.

Simply put, puppy mills are factory farms churning out mostly purebred dogs brokers sell to pet stores as well as online, or through newspaper ads and auctions. Most people don't realize that the cute little doggie in the pet store window may have severe health or behavioral problems that won't emerge till later. The breeding females suffer an even crueler fate, housed for their entire lives in crowded conditions with not enough food or water, virtually no exercise, and minimal human contact; when their breeding days are done, they're typically abandoned or killed. Even if they're taken to a shelter, they hardly ever get adopted because they're usually sick or too psychologically damaged.

Many commercial puppy mill operations stay in business for years, easily evading detection by the understaffed government regulatory agencies. But in the spring of 2007, one of the nation's worst cases was uncovered by inspectors in Nebraska. The facility, which had dogs cramped four and five to each tiny chickenwire cage, was quickly shut down—but there were 173 breeding dogs and puppies in dire shape. The Nebraska Humane Society stepped in and arranged prompt medical treatment—it's typical that puppy mill dogs need dental surgery because of gnawing on their enclosures, and knee surgery because of their overly crowded living quarters. Behavioral problems were another issue, and although many of the dogs were able to be fostered or put up for adoption, a few were in particularly bad shape. The Nebraska society turned to Best Friends, who agreed to take 10 of the dogs for the kind of rehabilitative care it does best.

ROSA, one of the 10 dogs rescued from a puppy mill in Nebraska and sent to Dogtown, was adopted early on but had a hard time adjusting to the only home she'd ever known. She was extremely withdrawn and basically stayed away from people. But her family persevered with love and care. Now Rosa lets her new mom Annie pick her up and shower her face with kisses. Dad Wayne doesn't quite get the same affection yet, but Rosa does let him pet her when they're up on the bed together.

ANIMAL poses in front of a mural in one of the offices at Dogtown (above, right). Muzzling was a necessity at first (above, with Sherry Woodard).

Spotlight on: Animal Who Became Noble

One of the 10 Nebraska Humane Society dogs was a fierce little terrier who almost didn't qualify as a domestic animal, so wild was his nature. The Best Friends team that traveled to Nebraska had picked him out because it was clear he needed a lot of help. He was in a large run with two other pups, and the Nebraska staff explained that he had already bitten people several times and was also prone to lashing out at the other dogs in his run, a behavior known as redirection (when a dog gets excited and doesn't know how to express it, he will typically attack the nearest thing he can get his teeth into). Once the terrier was at Dogtown, Sherry Woodard, Best Friends' behavior expert, decided to take him on as her special charge. She dubbed him Animal, after the muppet character of the same name.

Her first task was getting him cleaned up—his fur was matted with feces. Many dogs don't really enjoy getting bathed, but Animal had taken that dislike to a whole new level. The only way he knew to respond to any human contact was with his teeth. Sherry had to put on a pair of welding gloves, get a muzzle on him, and wrap him tight in a towel to keep him under control. He cried and thrashed during the whole process. His coat was in such bad shape that even the most thorough bath barely made a dent. Sherry realized he would have to be shaved, and the only way that was going to be possible was to wait until he was under anesthetic for his neutering.

Sherry began training Animal almost right away. She used two basic techniques: role modeling and positive reinforcement. Because Animal knew nothing about being a companion animal, Sherry brought her own dog, Miles, a paragon of good behavior, to all his training sessions. Animal was still out of control, but he would watch what Miles did, and during outdoor times he even started following Miles around, sniffing wherever Miles sniffed. As for the positive reinforcement, Sherry started very simply, offering Animal highly desirable treats from her hand. He wasn't yet close to taking one, but if he made any non-aggressive move toward her, she would praise him lavishly. When he did something unwanted, she would either ignore the behavior, distract him to do something else, or remove him from whatever in his environment was bringing out the negative behavior. Sherry was building a bond: "When you have a relationship with the dog, you have trust, and the dog wants to spend time with and work with you. By reinforcing behaviors that you like and want to

ANIMAL was so filthy that even the most thorough bathing couldn't clean him. He had to have much of his coat shorn off, something that could only be done while he was still under sedation from his neutering surgery.

75

continue seeing, you set the dog up for success."

Sherry and Animal's other caregivers also made a decision that might on the surface seem trivial: they would rename him. They had always planned to do so once the good personality they felt sure was in him came out. But now they decided it would be better to give him a name he could work toward; it would get everyone focused on a bright future instead of a troubled past. They solicited ideas from the Best Friends community, and a few weeks after his arrival, Animal became Noble.

Over the ensuing weeks, Noble made slow improvement. Careful exposure to unfamiliar dogs and people eventually got him into the habit of responding less than viciously. He was still watching Miles for guidance, but he wouldn't play with him nor with any of his toys. Then one day the caregivers received a big box of donated toys for the Nebraska puppies, and they decided to bring the dogs together to make their own choices. Kermit and Apple and Sweetums started sniffing at the toys, while Noble held back. Then another of the pups, a male named Gonzo, came in with his caregiver, and it was as if a switch had been thrown. Noble went up and greeted him happily, and the two started to romp. It was obvious they recognized each other, and although it had been important to keep the puppies apart so they would learn to start responding to people, this was clearly something Noble needed.

Shortly after, Sherry had to go out of town, so Noble started living in the Dogtown main office with other members of the training team, and he got time with Gonzo daily. He was also being introduced to more people and different surroundings, all of which would ultimately serve him well. There was no sugarcoating things, though: Noble had a long, long way to go. He was still fairly destructive, power cords being a favorite target; he hadn't made

NOBLE

Animal—now Noble—begins to show some of the dignity his caregivers hoped his new name would inspire. But it would be a long road. As Sherry Woodard puts it, "He displayed a curious combination of feisty, brave terrier and terrified dog."

Toys galore arrived for Animal/Noble and the other puppies rescued from the abusive puppy mill in Nebraska. Noble didn't know quite what to make of them at first. Now, in his forever home, he tussles happily with his playthings.

much progress on housetraining; and with unfamiliar dogs he tended to be a bully, despite his diminutive size. Caregivers did the best they could to keep him away from things he would destroy, and they continued to work on housetraining and all the other behavioral issues that stood in the way of Noble becoming an adoptable pet.

Jump forward to six months after Noble first came to Dogtown. Still a work in progress, Noble was nonetheless a little miracle of transformation. Housetraining had succeeded, destruction was on the wane, and most important of all, Noble had won his way into the heart of a woman from northern Utah who had adopted Kermit, another of the puppy-mill dogs, three months before. In January of 2008, he was on his way to his new forever home. There was a genuine nobility there where once had been a fierceness born of fear.

Progress and setbacks, frustrations and triumphs—such was the course of Noble's rehabilitation. Patience had again won the day, and it was as if, somehow or other, he had gotten the message that no one was going to give up on him, ever.

Such is the nature of the unconditional love that spreads throughout Dogtown, from sunrise to the quiet settling of twilight. Until that better place comes along—a loving family home— Dogtown remains, for dog after dog after dog, the best place to be.

A DOG'S BEST FRIEND

A Passion for Volunteering

She writes children's books for a living, and he illustrates them, but despite the satisfactions they get from their professional lives, true joy for Jeanne and Robin Modesitt comes from the many hours they devote to volunteering at Dogtown. Jeanne is there 20 hours a week, Robin 10, walking dogs and doing whatever they can to help Best Friends' professional staff. "We're able to lessen the load on the caregivers," Jeanne says, and at the same time they readily acknowledge that they're lifting burdens from their own hearts.

The Modesitts used to live in New Mexico with a little terrier named Bobo, who made it to 18 years old. When she died, they were devastated, and they knew they had to do something to get over their grief. "Then inside of us something stirred," Jeanne remembers, "and we felt we should go visit Best Friends. We had no idea why." They were members but had never been to the sanctuary, and at first they couldn't quite believe the beauty of the place, especially "the red cliffs, and that blue, blue sky." They spent three days walking dogs and soaking everything in. "Being around so many dogs, it just lifted us both," Jeanne says. "We realized it was mighty good medicine." The experience was so powerful that they decided to move to the area and become steady volunteers, something their work made possible.

They volunteer at The Lodges with some of the more difficult dogs. One of Jeanne's favorites was a pit bull named Joey, who had his share of troubles with aggression against other dogs. At Dogtown, though, he found a friend, a three-legged Labrador mix named Bryce, and the two of them were inseparable for almost 10 years. When Bryce died, Joey seemed as grief-stricken as the Modesitts had been over Bobo, so Jeanne reached out to him. She spent hours with him, not only walking but just being near him. Soon Joey was back to being a happy fellow, squealing with delight whenever he saw Jeanne. Today their special boy is a fellow named Ogy (above, giving Jeanne a kiss), whom they take for hour-long hikes almost every day. "He is a sweet boy," Jeanne says. "After our walks he just leans against us."

Jeanne thinks she can't quite articulate what's so special about Dogtown, but she's wrong. "It's this giant dog consciousness. All of those dogs—it helps you focus on the present, on the now, because that's where the dogs are at. They're not worried about tomorrow." Neither are the Modesitts. Tomorrow they know they'll be out on the trails again, walking with the dogs they care about so much.

79

Acknowledgments

The author wishes to thank the Best Friends photographers — Sarah Ause, Gary Kalpakoff, Clay Myers, Troy Snow, and Molly Wald — whose marvelous pictures bring the stories of Dogtown's dogs to life. Deep gratitude as well to all those at Best Friends — caregivers, vets, managers, and volunteers — who assisted in the creation of this book. Special thanks to Kate Hartson and Tina Taylor, longtime compatriots in the process of creating books, and to the wonderful people at Sellers Publishing. And, of course, the biggest thanks of all to the dogs!

In memory of Buddy and Duke.

Best Friends
ANIMAL SOCIETY

You can contact Best Friends at:
Best Friends Animal Society
5001 Angel Canyon Road
Kanab, Utah 84741

www.bestfriends.org
info@bestfriends.org
(435) 644-2001

How you can help
Become a part of Best Friends. You can sponsor one of the dogs or other animals who live at the sanctuary, or donate to the general work of the society, on the Best Friends Web site.

Volunteer at the sanctuary. Visit for a day or a week or longer. You can walk dogs, groom cats, feed horses, and much more.

Help in hundreds of other ways through the Best Friends network. See the Best Friends Web site for more information.

Adopt a pet from Best Friends or your local shelter Make sure your own pets are spayed or neutered.

NO MORE HOMELESS PETS